The Blueprint for a Fulfilling Life

Fulfilling Life

9 Essential Principles to Live By

Emma Brown

ISBN: 9798378583591

Contents

Introduction

In today's fast-paced world, it's easy to get lost in the daily grind and lose sight of the bigger picture. We often prioritize short-term goals over long-term aspirations and neglect to develop the skills and habits that lead to a fulfilling and successful life. In this book, we explore nine essential habits that can help anyone transform their life and achieve their goals.

From setting clear values and goals to practicing gratitude and contributing to something larger than yourself, each habit is presented with practical tips and examples to help readers implement them in their lives. We delve into the importance of developing skills such as communication, critical thinking, time management, problem-solving, financial management, leadership, adaptability, self-discipline, and creativity.

But perhaps the most important habit is the last one – contributing to something larger than yourself. It's easy to get wrapped up in our own lives and forget the impact we can have on the world around us. We examine why it's important to find ways to give back to our communities and work towards a greater good.

By incorporating these habits into our lives, we can become more productive, successful, and fulfilled. So whether you're a student, professional, or anyone looking to improve your life, this book has something to offer. Let's get started on the journey towards a better life!

Overview of the book

As a personal development coach, I believe that improving one's life requires a holistic approach that takes into account various aspects of one's well-being. Here are the top ten things to work on to improve your life:

Clarify your values: Understanding what's most important to you in life can help you make better decisions and prioritize your time and energy accordingly.

Develop a growth mindset: Adopting a growth mindset can help you approach challenges with a more positive attitude and embrace the learning opportunities that come with them.

Practice self-care: Taking care of your physical, emotional, and mental health is crucial for living a fulfilling life. This includes getting enough sleep, eating well, exercising regularly, and practicing relaxation techniques.

Build strong relationships: Cultivating healthy, supportive relationships with family, friends, and colleagues can have a profound impact on your well-being and happiness.

Develop emotional intelligence: Learning to manage your emotions, understand others' emotions, and communicate effectively can improve your relationships and help you navigate life's challenges more effectively.

Set goals: Having clear, specific goals can help you focus your efforts and stay motivated. Make sure your goals are realistic and align with your values.

Practice gratitude: Taking time to appreciate the good things in your life can improve your mood and help you stay positive, even during difficult times.

Learn new skills: Developing new skills can help you stay engaged and interested in life, and can also boost your confidence and enhance your career prospects.

Contribute to something larger than yourself: Engaging in activities that make a positive impact on others can give you a sense of purpose and meaning in life, and can also help you build a sense of community and connection with others.

Clarify your values

Identifying your core values can be an important step towards living a more authentic, fulfilling life. Here are three ways to clarify your values:

Reflect on what matters most to you

Take some time to think about the things that bring you the most happiness, fulfillment, and satisfaction in life. These could be things like spending time with loved ones, making a difference in the world, pursuing a passion, or achieving success in your career. Make a list of these things and try to identify common themes or values that underlie them.

John is a successful lawyer who works long hours and often feels stressed and exhausted. One day, he decides to take some time to reflect on what really matters to him in life. He starts by thinking about some of his happiest memories, and realizes that many of them involve spending time with his family and friends. He also remembers how much he enjoyed playing basketball in high school, and how it gave him a sense of purpose and belonging.

As he continues to reflect, John realizes that his values are closely tied to the relationships and activities that bring him joy and fulfillment. He writes down a list of the things that matter most to him: spending quality time with loved ones, making a positive impact in the world, staying active and healthy, and pursuing activities that he's passionate about.

With this newfound clarity, John decides to make some changes in his life. He starts setting aside more time for his family and friends, and takes up basketball again as a way to stay active and engaged in a hobby he enjoys. He also begins to look for ways to use his legal expertise to make a positive impact in his community, such as by volunteering at a local legal aid clinic.

By focusing on what matters most to him, John feels more fulfilled, energized, and aligned with his values.

Pay attention to your emotions

Our emotions can be powerful indicators of what's truly important to us. Notice when you feel particularly happy, fulfilled, or inspired, and try to identify what values are being expressed in those moments. Similarly, pay attention to times when you feel frustrated, unhappy, or unfulfilled, and consider what values might be missing or being violated in those situations.

Emma is a graphic designer who is feeling burnt out and unfulfilled in her job. One day, she decides to take a walk in the park during her lunch break to clear her head. As she's walking, she notices a group of children playing and laughing together. She feels a sense of warmth and happiness as she watches them, and realizes that she's been missing that feeling in her own life.

As she continues to reflect on this feeling, Emma realizes that what she's missing is a sense of playfulness, creativity, and spontaneity in her life. She realizes that her work has become too focused on deadlines and client demands, and that she's lost touch with the joy and excitement she used to feel about graphic design.

With this newfound awareness, Emma decides to make some changes in her life. She starts setting aside time for creative projects that she's passionate about, even if they don't pay as well as her design work. She also begins to seek out opportunities to work with clients who share her values and are more open to creative exploration.

By paying attention to her emotions and identifying what was missing in her life, Emma was able to clarify her values and take steps to align her work with those values. As a result, she feels more fulfilled and energized in her career.

Examine your actions

Our values are often reflected in the choices we make and the actions we take. Consider the times when you've felt most proud of yourself or the choices you've made, and think about what values were being expressed in those moments. On the other hand, consider times when you've made choices that didn't align with your values, and reflect on what might have led you to make those choices.

Louis is a recent college graduate who is struggling to find a job in his field. He's been feeling down and unmotivated, and has been spending a lot of time watching TV and playing video games to distract himself. One day, he decides to take a break from his usual routine and try something new. He signs up for a volunteer program at a local animal shelter.

As he spends time at the shelter, Louis realizes how much he enjoys working with animals and helping them find loving homes. He feels a sense of purpose and fulfillment that he hasn't felt in a long time. He also notices how good it feels to be part of a community of people who share his values of compassion and kindness.

Reflecting on his experience at the shelter, Louis realizes that he's been neglecting his values of compassion and community in his daily life. He hasn't been reaching out to his friends and family as much as he would like, and he hasn't been doing much to help others.

With this realization, Louis decides to make some changes in his life. He starts volunteering regularly at the animal shelter, and he also reaches out to some old friends to reconnect and strengthen his social connections. He feels more aligned with his values and more motivated to pursue a career that aligns with his passion for animals.

-

Once you have a better understanding of your core values, you can prioritize them in a few ways:

Create a values hierarchy

Consider which values are most important to you and rank them in order of priority. This can help you make decisions more easily and ensure that you're spending your time and energy on the things that matter most.

For example:

Health and wellness - I prioritize taking care of my physical and mental health, including regular exercise, healthy eating, and mindfulness practices.

Family and relationships - I value my connections with my loved ones and prioritize spending quality time with them, nurturing those relationships, and being there for them when they need me.

Personal growth - I am committed to continuous learning and growth, whether it's through reading, attending workshops, or seeking feedback and coaching.

Creativity and self-expression - I value expressing myself creatively, whether through writing, music, or other forms of artistic expression.

Integrity and honesty - I believe in being honest and truthful in all my interactions, and I value people who have a strong sense of integrity and honor their commitments.

Community involvement - I believe in giving back to my community and contributing to the greater good through volunteering and other forms of service.

Financial stability - While money is not my top priority, I recognize the importance of financial stability and take steps to manage my money wisely and plan for my future.

By creating a values hierarchy, I can use this as a guide when making decisions and setting goals. When faced with a choice or opportunity, I can refer to this hierarchy to ensure that I'm making choices that align with my most deeply held values.

Align your goals with your values

When setting goals for yourself, make sure they align with your core values. This can help you stay motivated and focused on the things that are most important to you.

Lise is a teacher who is feeling unfulfilled in her job and wants to set some new goals to move her career in a more satisfying direction. She starts by reflecting on her values, and identifies the following as her top values: making a positive impact, creativity and self-expression, personal growth, family and relationships, financial stability, and health and wellness.

She then examines her current goals and asks herself which ones align with these values:

Aligned goals:

- Enroll in a graduate program in education to deepen her knowledge and skills as a teacher, aligning with her value of personal growth.
- Start a blog where she can share her ideas about innovative teaching strategies and connect with other educators, aligning with her value of creativity and self-expression.
- Take a sabbatical from teaching to travel and spend more time with her family, aligning with her value of family and relationships.

Goals that are not aligned:

- Accept a promotion to a leadership position in her school district, which would require her to work longer hours and take on administrative responsibilities that don't align with her values of personal growth and creativity.
- Teach summer school to earn extra money, even though it would interfere with her plans to spend time with her family and pursue her other goals.
- Participate in a research study on a teaching method she disagrees with, just to earn some extra income, even though it conflicts with her value of making a positive impact.

With this awareness, Lise decides to focus on her aligned goals and let go of the ones that don't align with her values. She enrolls in the graduate program, starts her blog, and takes a sabbatical to travel and spend time with her family. By aligning her goals with her values, Lise feels more fulfilled, motivated, and energized in her career.

Use your values as a guide for decision-making

When faced with difficult decisions, consider how each option aligns with your values. This can help you make choices that feel authentic and true to who you are.

Julie is a college student who has been offered a summer internship in her field of study, but the internship is located across the country and she would have to spend the summer living in a city where she knows no one. Julie has always valued family and relationships, and she's torn between wanting to take this opportunity to advance her career and feeling guilty about leaving her family for the summer.

To use her values as a guide for decision-making, Julie asks herself the following questions:

How does this decision align with my values? She recognizes that the internship aligns with her value of personal growth and career advancement, but conflicts with her value of family and relationships.

How will this decision impact my relationships with others? She considers how her family will react to her decision, and whether they will feel hurt or resentful if she chooses to leave for the summer. She also thinks about how the decision will affect her own relationships and connections in her current community.

How will this decision impact my overall well-being? She considers the potential stress and loneliness of spending a summer in a new place with no support system, as well as the potential benefits to her mental and emotional health from taking on a new challenge and pursuing her career goals.

After weighing these factors, Julie decides that she values her personal growth and career goals enough to take the internship, but she also wants to honor her commitment to her family and maintain her relationships with them. She decides to stay in touch with her family regularly through phone calls and video chats, and to plan a family vacation at the end of the summer to reconnect and spend quality time together. By using her values as a guide for decision-making, Julie is able to make a difficult decision with greater clarity and confidence.

Develop a growth mindset

Here are three things you can do to adopt and develop a growth mindset:

Embrace challenges

Challenge yourself to step outside of your comfort zone and try new things, even if they are difficult or uncomfortable. Rather than fearing failure or feeling discouraged when you make mistakes, approach challenges as opportunities for growth and learning. Focus on the process of learning and improving, rather than on the end result.

Charles is a graphic designer who has been working in the same job for several years. He feels like he has reached a plateau in his career and is no longer feeling challenged by his work. Charles recognizes that in order to grow and develop as a designer, he needs to push himself out of his comfort zone and take on new challenges.

To embrace this challenge, Charles decides to enroll in an online course on a new design software that he has never used before. The course is advanced and he knows it will be challenging, but he is excited to learn something new and expand his skills.

As he starts the course, Charles quickly realizes that he has a lot to learn and that the software is more complex than he had anticipated. However, he doesn't get discouraged or give up. Instead, he focuses on the process of learning and improving, recognizing that it's natural to struggle when taking on something new. He sets aside time each day to work on the course, breaks down the material into manageable chunks, and asks for help when he needs it.

After several weeks of hard work, Charles completes the course and feels a great sense of accomplishment. He has not only learned a new skill, but he has also developed a growth mindset that will help him tackle future challenges with confidence and resilience.

By embracing challenges and seeking out new experiences, Charles has been able to develop his skills and grow as a designer. He has also learned the value of persistence, hard work, and a positive attitude in achieving his goals.

Cultivate a positive mindset

Train yourself to think positively about challenges and setbacks, rather than getting stuck in negative self-talk or a fixed mindset. Recognize that setbacks and failures are a natural part of the learning process, and that they can provide valuable lessons and insights. Use positive affirmations and visualization techniques to build your confidence and resilience.

Cathy is a shy girl who often feels anxious in social situations. She tends to get caught up in negative self-talk and worries about what others think of her. However, Cathy recognizes that her shyness is holding her back and preventing her from reaching her full potential.

To cultivate a positive mindset, Cathy decides to start practicing daily affirmations. Each morning, she looks in the mirror and tells herself positive statements such as, "I am capable," "I am worthy," and "I am confident." At first, Cathy feels silly doing this, but over time she begins to believe in these positive affirmations and they become a part of her self-talk.

Cathy also starts visualizing positive outcomes for social situations she is anxious about. For example, before a party, she imagines herself having fun and engaging in interesting conversations with others. By visualizing positive outcomes, she is able to shift her mindset from one of anxiety to one of excitement and anticipation.

Finally, Cathy seeks out support from a friend or mentor who can provide her with positive feedback and encouragement. This person reminds her of her strengths and accomplishments, and helps her to see her shyness as a challenge to be overcome, rather than a fixed trait.

Through these practices, Cathy is able to cultivate a more positive mindset and develop a growth mindset. She learns to focus on her strengths and abilities, rather than her weaknesses and fears, and to approach social situations with a sense of curiosity and openness. Over time, her confidence and resilience grow, and she is able to overcome her shyness and achieve her goals.

Seek out feedback and support

Surround yourself with people who will challenge you to grow and learn, and seek out constructive feedback from them. Recognize that feedback is a valuable tool for learning and improving, and use it to identify areas where you can focus your efforts. Be open to new perspectives and ideas, and be willing to make adjustments to your approach as needed.

David is a man who has always prided himself on being self-sufficient. He enjoys taking on new challenges and figuring things out on his own, without asking for help or feedback. However, David has come to realize that this approach is limiting his growth and development.

To seek out feedback and support, David decides to join a local business group where he can connect with other entrepreneurs and receive guidance from experienced mentors. At first, he feels uncomfortable asking for advice and sharing his struggles, but he soon realizes the value of seeking out the perspectives of others.

Through this group, David is able to receive feedback on his ideas and projects, as well as gain new insights and perspectives. He also connects with a mentor who provides him with guidance and support as he navigates the challenges of entrepreneurship. With this feedback and support, David is able to make more informed decisions and take his business to the next level.

David also seeks out feedback from his team members and colleagues. Instead of always assuming that he knows best, he asks for their input and suggestions on how to improve processes and solve problems. This not only helps him to improve his own skills, but also creates a culture of collaboration and openness within his organization.

Through these practices, David is able to develop a growth mindset and recognize the value of seeking out feedback and support. He learns that by connecting with others and asking for help when he needs it, he can overcome his own limitations and achieve greater success.

-

By adopting a growth mindset and focusing on personal growth and development, you can increase your resilience, confidence, and motivation, and achieve greater success in all areas of your life.

Practice self-care

Here are some specific ways to practice self-care in terms of physical, emotional, and mental health:

Physical health:

Get enough sleep: Sleep is crucial for physical health, so aim for 7-9 hours of sleep each night.

According to several studies, sleep deprivation can have negative effects on cognitive performance, mood, physical health, and overall well-being. For example, one study found that even short-term sleep deprivation can result in poorer cognitive performance, while another study found that sleep deprivation can negatively affect mood and increase the risk of depression. These findings underscore the importance of getting enough sleep for our overall health and well-being.

Exercise regularly: Regular physical activity can help you maintain a healthy weight, reduce your risk of chronic diseases, and improve your mood. Aim for at least 30 minutes of moderate exercise each day.

Here are a few basic exercises that can be done anywhere and don't require any special equipment:

- **Walking**: Walking is a great way to get some exercise and fresh air. You can start with a short walk around your neighborhood and gradually increase your distance and speed as your fitness level improves.

- **Squats**: Squats are a great exercise for strengthening your legs and glutes. Stand with your feet shoulder-width apart and slowly lower your body as if you're sitting in a chair. Keep your weight on your heels and your knees behind your toes. Straighten back up to a standing position and repeat.

- **Push-ups**: Push-ups are a great exercise for strengthening your chest, shoulders, and triceps. Start in a plank position with your hands shoulder-width apart and your body in a straight line. Lower your body until your chest nearly touches the ground, then push back up to the starting position.

- **Plank**: Planking is an excellent exercise for building core strength. Start in a push-up position with your arms extended and your body in a straight line. Hold this position for as long as you can, making sure to keep your abs engaged and your hips level.

- **Jumping jacks**: Jumping jacks are a simple, effective exercise for getting your heart rate up and improving your cardiovascular fitness. Stand with your feet together and your arms at your sides. Jump your feet out to shoulder-width apart while raising your arms overhead, then jump back to the starting position.

Eat a healthy diet: Focus on eating a balanced diet that includes plenty of fruits, vegetables, whole grains, lean protein, and healthy fats.

Here are a few examples of balanced meals for breakfast, lunch, and dinner:

Breakfast:

- Oatmeal with sliced banana, chopped walnuts, and a drizzle of honey
- Greek yogurt with mixed berries, granola, and a drizzle of maple syrup
- Whole grain toast with avocado, a poached egg, and a sprinkle of salt and pepper

Lunch:

- Grilled chicken breast with roasted vegetables (such as broccoli, bell peppers, and onions) and quinoa
- Spinach salad with grilled shrimp, cherry tomatoes, sliced almonds, and a balsamic vinaigrette

- Lentil soup with a side of whole grain crackers and sliced apple

Dinner:

- Baked salmon with roasted sweet potato and steamed green beans
- Grilled tofu with stir-fried mixed vegetables (such as bell peppers, carrots, and snow peas) and brown rice
- Spaghetti with turkey meatballs, a side salad, and a slice of whole grain bread

The general idea is to aim for a mix of lean protein, complex carbohydrates, healthy fats, and plenty of fruits and vegetables. It's also important to stay hydrated throughout the day by drinking plenty of water.

Practice good hygiene: Taking care of your personal hygiene can help you feel good about yourself and prevent the spread of germs.

This is important not just for health but also for self-confidence and wellbeing. There are many natural and environmentally friendly ways to do this. Here are a few tips:

- Use natural soap: Choose a soap that is made from natural ingredients and free from harsh chemicals.

Look for products that contain ingredients like coconut oil, shea butter, and essential oils.

- Use natural deodorant: Traditional deodorants often contain aluminum, which has been linked to health concerns. Look for natural deodorants that are made with baking soda, coconut oil, and essential oils.

- Use a natural toothpaste: Conventional toothpaste often contains fluoride, which can be harmful if ingested in large amounts. Look for natural toothpastes that are fluoride-free and contain natural ingredients like baking soda, xylitol, and essential oils.

- Use natural shampoo and conditioner: Traditional hair care products often contain sulfates and other harsh chemicals that can strip the hair of its natural oils. Look for natural shampoos and conditioners that are made with gentle ingredients like aloe vera, coconut oil, and chamomile.

- Use natural skincare products: Many conventional skincare products contain synthetic fragrances, preservatives, and other harsh chemicals. Look for natural products that are free from these ingredients and contain natural moisturizers like shea butter, jojoba oil, and aloe vera.

- Practice good oral hygiene: In addition to using a natural toothpaste, it's important to floss daily and brush your teeth at least twice a day. You can also try oil pulling, which involves swishing coconut oil in your mouth for several minutes to remove bacteria and freshen your breath.

Everyone's personal hygiene routine will be unique to their needs and preferences. Find products and practices that work for you and make you feel good.

Emotional health:

Practice mindfulness: Mindfulness involves paying attention to the present moment without judgment. It can help you reduce stress and increase your sense of well-being.

Here's an example of a simple mindfulness meditation session:

- Find a quiet and comfortable place where you can sit or lie down without being disturbed. You can sit in a chair or cross-legged on a cushion or mat, or lie down on a yoga mat or comfortable surface.

- Close your eyes and take a few deep breaths, focusing on the sensation of the air moving in and out of your body. Allow your thoughts to come and go without judgment.

- Bring your attention to the present moment, focusing on the sensations in your body. Start at the top of your head and work your way down, noticing any areas of tension or discomfort.

- Once you've scanned your body, bring your attention to your breath. Notice the sensation of the air moving in and out of your body. If your mind starts to wander, gently bring your attention back to your breath.

- As you continue to focus on your breath, you may notice thoughts or feelings arising. Acknowledge these thoughts without judgment and then let them go, returning your focus to your breath.

- Continue to focus on your breath for several minutes, allowing yourself to relax and become more present in the moment.

- When you're ready, gently open your eyes and take a few deep breaths before getting up and resuming your day.

Mindfulness meditation is a practice that takes time and patience. It's normal for your mind to wander, and the goal is not to eliminate all thoughts but to simply observe them without judgment. By practicing mindfulness regularly, you can learn to be more present and aware in your daily life.

Connect with others: Spending time with friends and loved ones can help you feel supported and reduce feelings of isolation.

It's important to respect your need for alone time, but it's also important to maintain social connections for your overall well-being. Here are a few tips for connecting with others when you want to be alone:

- Schedule social time: You can set aside specific times or days for socializing so that you can plan your alone time around them. This can help you feel more in control of your schedule and avoid feeling overwhelmed by social obligations.

- Join a group or club: Consider joining a group or club that aligns with your interests or hobbies. This way, you can connect with others who share your passions and engage in activities that you enjoy.

- Communicate your needs: It's important to communicate your need for alone time to your friends and loved ones so that they can understand and respect your boundaries. You can explain that you still value your relationship with them and want to stay connected, but that you also need some time to yourself.

- Try online connections: If you're not up for in-person interactions, consider joining an online community or forum. You can connect with others who share your interests or struggles without having to leave the comfort of your own home.

It's okay to need alone time, but social connections are still important for your overall well-being. By finding a balance between your need for solitude and your need for social connections, you can maintain a healthy and fulfilling life.

Pursue hobbies and interests: Engaging in activities you enjoy can help you relax and reduce stress.

I have a cousin who was always a bundle of nerves, to the point where we sometimes nicknamed him among ourselves "Worrywart." However, he recently discovered the joys of gardening and it has made a tremendous difference in his life. He now spends hours in his garden each week, cultivating and caring for his plants. This hobby has given him a sense of purpose and fulfillment that he was missing before, and has helped to calm his anxious mind.

In addition to the mental and emotional benefits, gardening has also given him a new physical activity to enjoy. He spends time outdoors in the fresh air and sunshine, which is great for his overall health and well-being.

Through pursuing this new hobby, my cousin has been able to improve his mental, emotional, and physical health. It just goes to show that finding a new hobby or interest can have a transformative effect on one's life.

Practice gratitude: Taking time to reflect on the things you are grateful for can help you cultivate a positive outlook and increase your overall happiness.

Here's an example of a list of things for which a person can feel gratitude:

- My health and the health of my loved ones.
- Having a job that allows me to provide for myself and my family.
- Having a safe and comfortable place to live.
- Access to clean water and nutritious food.
- The beauty of nature and the changing seasons.
- Supportive and loving relationships with family and friends.
- Access to education and opportunities for personal growth.
- The ability to travel and experience different cultures.
- Moments of joy and laughter that bring light to my life.

- The ability to help others and make a positive impact in the world.

Gratitude is all about focusing on the good things in life, even during difficult times. By regularly practicing gratitude and reflecting on the things we are thankful for, we can cultivate a more positive outlook and improve our overall well-being.

Mental health:

Manage stress: There are many ways to manage stress, including exercise, mindfulness, and relaxation techniques like deep breathing or progressive muscle relaxation.

When I feel stressed, one of my favorite techniques is to practice deep breathing. I find a quiet spot where I won't be disturbed, sit or lie down comfortably, and then focus on my breath. I inhale deeply through my nose, hold it for a few seconds, and then exhale slowly through my mouth. I repeat this for a few minutes until I feel my body start to relax and my mind calm down. This simple technique helps me to manage my stress and anxiety in a natural and effective way, and I find that it can be done anytime, anywhere, which makes it a very convenient option for me.

Seek professional help if needed: If you are struggling with a mental health issue, don't hesitate to seek help from a mental health professional.

A former neighbor of my mother struggled with anxiety and depression for years, but was hesitant to seek professional help. She tried to manage her symptoms on her own by reading self-help books and making lifestyle changes, but nothing seemed to work. It wasn't until a friend convinced her to see a therapist that she started to make real progress. With the help of her therapist, she was able to identify the underlying causes of her anxiety and depression and develop strategies to manage her symptoms. Seeking professional help can be a difficult step, but it can be life-changing for those who struggle with mental health issues. There is no shame in asking for help, and that there are professionals who are trained to help people overcome their struggles.

Practice self-compassion: Be kind and understanding toward yourself, especially during difficult times.

We sometimes tend to be hard and merciless on ourselves, especially when we make mistakes or face failures. Instead of being kind and understanding with ourselves, we often criticize and judge ourselves harshly, which can lead to negative emotions and a decrease in self-esteem. Practicing self-compassion involves treating ourselves with the same kindness and understanding that we would offer to a good friend who is struggling.

One way to practice self-compassion is to reframe negative self-talk into positive self-talk. For example, instead of berating yourself for a mistake, you could say to yourself, "I made a mistake, but it doesn't define me as a person." You can also practice self-compassion by engaging in self-care activities, such as taking a relaxing bath or reading a good book. Additionally, it can be helpful to remind yourself that everyone makes mistakes and experiences failures, and that it's a natural part of the learning and growing process. By practicing self-compassion, you can learn to be kinder and more patient with yourself, which can improve your mental health and overall well-being.

Set boundaries: Setting boundaries can help you manage your time and prioritize your needs, which can improve your mental health.

Here are some examples of boundaries that can be set:

- Time boundaries: Setting specific times during the day for work and personal life, and not allowing work to intrude on personal time or vice versa.

- Emotional boundaries: Recognizing and respecting your own emotions, and not allowing others to manipulate or control them.

- Physical boundaries: Setting limits on physical touch and personal space, and not allowing others to make you uncomfortable or violated.

- Communication boundaries: Being clear and direct in your communication, and not allowing others to speak to you in a disrespectful or abusive way.

- Material boundaries: Being clear about what you are willing to share or lend, and not allowing others to take advantage of your possessions or finances.

The specific boundaries that you set will depend on your personal values and needs.

Build strong relationships

Here are three prioritized points for building strong relationships:

Be present and attentive

One of the most important ways to build strong relationships is by being present and attentive when spending time with loved ones or colleagues. This means actively listening, showing interest in their lives, and offering support when needed. It's important to avoid distractions like phones or other devices, and to make an effort to connect on a personal level.

Samantha and Maria have been best friends since childhood. Despite living in different cities now, they make an effort to catch up regularly over the phone. One day, Samantha calls Maria in tears, feeling overwhelmed and stressed from work. Maria immediately senses that her friend needs support and puts aside whatever she was doing to give Samantha her full attention. She listens attentively, offering kind words and understanding. After their conversation, Samantha feels comforted and grateful for the strong bond she has with her friend, who took the time to be present and supportive during a difficult time.

Now, imagine if Maria had not been present and attentive during their meeting. Instead, she could have easily been distracted by her own phone or thoughts, or dismissed her friend's situation as trivial or unimportant. She may have felt even more alone and unsupported in her time of need, potentially leading to a further spiral of negative emotions and actions.

By being present and attentive, Maria not only provided a listening ear and a shoulder to cry on, but also demonstrated her care and concern for her friend's well-being. This act of support could have a lasting impact on their relationship, strengthening their bond and trust in each other. It's a small but powerful reminder of the importance of being present and attentive in our relationships, and the positive impact it can have on those we care about.

Communicate openly and honestly

Healthy relationships require honest and open communication. This means being able to express your feelings and needs in a clear and respectful way, while also being receptive to the feelings and needs of others. Avoiding conflict or avoiding difficult conversations can lead to misunderstandings and resentment, so it's important to address issues as they arise.

Communicating openly and honestly can be challenging, but there are several techniques that can help:

- **Use "I" statements**: Instead of blaming or accusing the other person, focus on your own feelings and needs. For example, instead of saying "You never listen to me," say "I feel frustrated when I don't feel heard."

- **Active listening**: Make an effort to truly understand the other person's perspective. Reflect back what they've said to show that you're listening and ask questions to clarify any misunderstandings.

- **Avoid defensiveness**: When the other person says something that triggers a defensive response, take a step back and try to understand where they're coming from. Respond calmly and avoid attacking or blaming them.

- **Practice empathy**: Put yourself in the other person's shoes and try to understand their feelings and needs. This can help you respond in a more compassionate and understanding way.

- **Be clear and direct**: Speak honestly and clearly, but also be respectful and diplomatic. Don't beat around the bush or use passive-aggressive language.

- **Practice patience**: Good communication takes time and effort, and it's not always easy. Be patient and understanding, and don't expect immediate results.

Foster trust and respect

Trust and respect are essential components of strong relationships. Trust is built over time through consistent behavior and follow-through, while respect is shown through treating others with kindness and consideration. When trust and respect are present, relationships are more likely to thrive and withstand challenging times. It's important to be dependable and reliable, and to avoid betraying trust or violating boundaries.

Here are three ways to gain people's trust:

Be consistent: Consistency is key to building trust. Do what you say you will do, and follow through on your commitments. This shows that you are reliable and trustworthy.

Listen actively: When someone speaks to you, give them your full attention. Ask questions and show genuine interest in what they are saying. This demonstrates that you value their thoughts and feelings and are invested in the relationship.

Be honest: Always be truthful, even if it's difficult. People are more likely to trust someone who is honest and transparent, even if the truth is not always what they want to hear.

Here are three things NOT to do in order to gain people's trust:

Don't lie or deceive: People can sense when someone is not being honest with them, and this can quickly erode trust.

Don't break promises or commitments: If you say you'll do something, follow through. When you fail to keep your word, it can damage your credibility and trustworthiness.

Don't gossip or spread rumors: When you engage in gossip or spread rumors about others, it can make people question your judgment and your ability to keep things confidential.

Here are three ways to gain respect:

Treat others with respect: To gain respect, you must first give it. Treat others as you would like to be treated. Show kindness, empathy, and consideration to everyone, regardless of their position or background.

Be confident: Confidence is key to earning respect. Believe in yourself and your abilities, and others will believe in you too. Speak up when you have something to say, and don't be afraid to take charge when the situation calls for it.

Demonstrate competence: People are more likely to respect someone who is skilled and knowledgeable in their field. Continuously work to improve your skills and knowledge, and show others that you are a capable and competent individual.

And here are three things NOT to do in order to gain respect:

Don't be disrespectful to others: If you want others to respect you, you need to treat them with respect as well. Being rude or dismissive can quickly erode any respect you may have earned.

Don't be inconsistent or unreliable: If you're not consistent in your actions and behavior, it can be difficult for others to take you seriously and respect you as a reliable and trustworthy individual.

Don't act entitled or arrogant: If you act like you're better than others or entitled to special treatment, it can turn people off and make them less likely to respect you. Show humility and gratitude, and recognize that everyone has something valuable to offer.

Develop emotional intelligence

Here are three main things you can do to develop emotional intelligence:

Practice self-awareness

To manage your emotions, it's important to first understand them. Take some time to reflect on your emotions and how they affect your behavior. Try to identify what triggers certain emotions, and how you typically respond to those triggers. Pay attention to your body's physical reactions to emotions as well, such as muscle tension or heart rate.

There are exercises that can help you identify what triggers your emotions. One such exercise is called the "ABC" exercise, which stands for "Activating Event, Beliefs, and Consequences." Here's how to do it:

Activating Event: Identify the event that triggered your emotions. Write down the details of the event, including who was involved, where it happened, and what exactly happened.

Beliefs: Write down the beliefs or thoughts you had about the event. These are the things you told yourself about the event, and they can be either rational or irrational.

Consequences: Write down the emotional and behavioral consequences that resulted from your beliefs about the event. This includes the emotions you felt and the actions you took as a result of those emotions.

By completing this exercise, you can begin to identify the triggers for your emotions and understand the thoughts and beliefs that are contributing to those emotions. This can help you to better manage your emotions and communicate effectively with others.

Practice empathy

Understanding the emotions of others is a key component of emotional intelligence. Practice active listening to understand the feelings and perspectives of those around you. Try to put yourself in their shoes and imagine how you would feel in their situation. Avoid making judgments or assumptions about their feelings.

Imagine that you're having a conversation with a close friend who is going through a difficult time. You want to support them and show that you understand how they're feeling. To practice active listening, you could try the following:

Pay attention: Give your friend your full attention, put away any distractions like your phone, and maintain eye contact. Show them that you are fully present and ready to listen.

Listen for understanding: As your friend talks, focus on understanding their perspective. Try to put yourself in their shoes and imagine how they might be feeling. Avoid interrupting or giving advice too quickly.

Reflect and clarify: Repeat back what you hear to ensure that you have understood your friend's message correctly. Paraphrase what they said to show that you are actively listening and interested in understanding their feelings.

For example, if your friend says, "I feel so alone and isolated right now," you might say, "It sounds like you're really struggling with feeling disconnected from others. Can you tell me more about what's been going on?"

By practicing active listening, you can build a deeper connection with your friend and show that you care about their feelings.

Practice effective communication

Clear communication is crucial for developing emotional intelligence. Practice expressing your emotions in a constructive way, using "I" statements instead of "you" statements. Practice active listening to understand the emotions and perspectives of others, and respond in a way that acknowledges their feelings. Avoid interrupting, assuming or minimizing their emotions.

Here's six Tips for Effective Communication:

Spend most of your time asking questions and gathering information about the other person's interests, concerns, and priorities, rather than just advocating your own point of view.

Use clear and direct language, avoiding jargon and acronyms.

Be prepared and organized when presenting your ideas, focusing on your interests, concerns, and priorities. Anticipate the other party's questions and have answers ready.

Be curious, listen actively, and ask questions to understand the other person's requests and demands. Avoid making demands and focus on making requests instead.

Be aware of your body language and tone of voice, as they can be just as important as the words you use. Avoid behaviors that can be interpreted as aggressive, and be culturally sensitive to non-verbal communication.

Use objective criteria such as industry practices, regulations, policies, and precedents, to create neutral ground for analyzing options.

Set goals

Here are three ways to <u>set</u> goals in line with our values and stick to them:

Identify your core values: In order to set goals in line with your values, you first need to identify what those values are. As we saw in Chapter 1, think about what is most important to you in life and what you want to prioritize. Your goals should align with your values and reflect what is most meaningful to you.

Make your goals specific and measurable: When setting goals, it's important to be specific about what you want to achieve and how you plan to measure your progress. Make sure your goals are SMART (Specific, Measurable, Achievable, Relevant, and Time-bound). This will help you stay focused on what you want to achieve and make it easier to track your progress.

Develop a plan of action: Once you've identified your goals, create a plan of action that outlines the steps you need to take to achieve them. Break down your goals into smaller, more manageable tasks and assign deadlines for each one. This will make it easier to stay on track and hold yourself accountable.

To <u>stick</u> to your goals, consider the following:

Hold yourself accountable: One of the most important factors in achieving your goals is holding yourself accountable. This means taking responsibility for your actions and making a commitment to follow through on your goals. Keep track of your progress and be honest with yourself about what's working and what's not.

Stay motivated: Motivation can be a key factor in achieving your goals. Find ways to stay motivated, whether that's through visualization, positive self-talk, or rewards for achieving milestones. Remember why you set your goals in the first place and keep that in mind when you face challenges or obstacles.

Be flexible: It's important to be flexible when working towards your goals. Sometimes unexpected challenges or opportunities may arise that require you to adjust your plans. Don't be afraid to modify your goals or your plan of action if necessary, as long as it still aligns with your values and ultimate objectives.

Some common objectives:

Here are 10 goal ideas that most people can consider to improve their well-being and life:

- Improve physical health: Set goals to exercise regularly, eat a healthy diet, get enough sleep, and take care of any health issues.

- Learn a new skill: Choose a skill you've always wanted to learn and set goals to acquire it, such as playing an instrument, learning a new language, or acquiring a professional certification.

- Travel to new places: Set goals to visit new cities, states, or countries to expand your worldview, experience new cultures, and create memories.

- Read more: Set goals to read a certain number of books per month or per year, or to read specific books that will help you grow personally or professionally.

- Volunteer or give back: Set goals to volunteer at a local organization or donate a portion of your income to a cause that aligns with your values.

- Improve relationships: Set goals to strengthen relationships with family, friends, or colleagues by spending more quality time with them, being more present and attentive, and being a good listener.

- Learn to manage stress: Set goals to incorporate stress-management techniques like meditation, deep breathing, or yoga into your daily routine.

- Save money: Set financial goals to save a certain amount of money each month, pay off debt, or invest in your future.

- Pursue a passion: Set goals to pursue a hobby or passion that brings you joy, such as painting, writing, or playing sports.

- Develop a positive mindset: Set goals to practice positive self-talk, cultivate gratitude, and focus on the good in life rather than dwelling on negativity or setbacks.

Some common BAD goals:

- Trying to impress others at all costs
- Pursuing material possessions beyond what is reasonable or necessary
- Engaging in risky or harmful behaviors for the sake of excitement
- Seeking revenge or harboring grudges
- Trying to control or manipulate others
- Obsessing over perfection in oneself or others

- Focusing solely on career success at the expense of personal relationships and well-being
- Maintaining toxic or unhealthy relationships
- Neglecting personal growth and self-improvement
- Holding onto limiting beliefs or negative self-talk.

While achieving goals is important for personal growth and success, the act of setting goals can be just as valuable because it forces individuals to clarify their values, motivations, and priorities, helps them to focus their efforts and attention, and gives them a sense of direction and purpose. In this way, even if a goal is not achieved, the process of setting it can still lead to growth and positive change. Additionally, the act of striving for a goal can often bring about unexpected opportunities and experiences that may be just as valuable or even more valuable than the original goal itself. Therefore, setting and pursuing meaningful goals can lead to personal fulfillment and growth, regardless of whether they are ultimately achieved or not.

Practice gratitude

There are several ways to develop a feeling of gratitude:

Keep a gratitude journal: Take time each day to write down a few things you're grateful for. It could be something as simple as a warm cup of tea or a kind word from a friend. Focusing on the positive things in your life can help shift your mindset to a more grateful one.

Practice mindfulness: Mindfulness meditation involves focusing your attention on the present moment and accepting it without judgment. By focusing on the present moment, you can appreciate the good things that are happening right now instead of always looking for what's next.

Express your gratitude: Tell someone how much you appreciate them or thank them for something they've done for you. By expressing your gratitude to others, you can strengthen your relationships and increase your own feelings of happiness.

Volunteer your time: Giving back to others can help you appreciate what you have and develop a sense of gratitude.

Volunteer at a local shelter, participate in a beach clean-up, or donate your time to a non-profit organization.

Surround yourself with positive influences: Spend time with people who are positive, uplifting, and grateful. This can help reinforce a grateful mindset and make it easier to cultivate gratitude in your own life.

Remember, developing a feeling of gratitude takes time and practice. Start small and be patient with yourself as you work to shift your mindset.

A gratitude meditation

Here's an example of a gratitude meditation:

- Find a comfortable and quiet place to sit or lie down.

- Close your eyes and take a few deep breaths to relax.

- Bring to mind something or someone in your life that you are grateful for. It can be a person, a place, a thing, a memory, or anything else that brings up feelings of gratitude.

- Focus on that feeling of gratitude and allow it to grow in your heart and mind. Imagine that feeling spreading throughout your body and filling you up with warmth and joy.

- Take a few deep breaths and say to yourself, "Thank you for this moment of gratitude and peace."

- Repeat the process with as many things or people that you are grateful for as you like.

- When you're ready, slowly open your eyes and take a moment to reflect on how you feel.

This meditation can be practiced for just a few minutes or as long as you like, and can be a powerful way to cultivate a daily gratitude practice.

A prayer of gratitude

Here is an example of a prayer of gratitude:

"Dear [God/Universe/Spirit/Higher Power],

I want to take a moment to express my gratitude for all the blessings in my life. I am grateful for the roof over my head, the food on my table, and the people who love and support me. I am grateful for my health and the ability to experience the beauty of nature around me. I am grateful for the opportunities and challenges that have helped me grow and learn.

Thank you for all the small and big things in my life that bring me joy, peace, and happiness. Help me to remember the abundance in my life and to appreciate it every day. May I never take any of it for granted.

Amen/So be it/And so it is."

Learn new skills

Learning new skills is essential for personal and professional growth. It helps to expand your knowledge, build your confidence, and open up new opportunities. One of the best ways to learn a new skill is through deliberate practice. This means breaking down the skill into smaller parts and focusing on improving each part, one at a time. Additionally, seeking out a mentor or taking a class can provide guidance and support in your learning journey.

For example, if you want to learn how to play the guitar, you can start by learning the basic chords and practicing them one at a time. Once you have a grasp on the chords, you can start to work on transitioning between them smoothly. Finding a guitar teacher or joining a beginner's guitar class can help you learn proper technique and give you feedback on your progress. With consistent practice and dedication, you can continue to build on your skills and eventually become a proficient guitar player.

Some essential skills

Here are some essential skills that every person should have:

Communication: The ability to express oneself clearly and effectively is essential in every aspect of life.

The best way to learn to communicate better is to practice actively listening and being aware of your own communication style. This means paying close attention to both verbal and nonverbal communication, such as body language and tone of voice, and being mindful of how these elements impact the message you are trying to convey.

Another important aspect of improving communication is being open to feedback and willing to make changes based on that feedback. This can involve seeking out feedback from others, reflecting on past communication experiences, and working to make adjustments as needed.

In addition, developing strong communication skills often requires a willingness to step outside of your comfort zone and try new approaches to communicating. This might involve taking courses or workshops on communication, reading books or articles on the subject, or seeking out mentors or coaches who can offer guidance and support.

Ultimately, the key to becoming a better communicator is to approach communication as a skill that can be improved with practice and a willingness to learn and grow. By being intentional about your communication and taking steps to improve it, you can build stronger relationships, advance your career, and achieve greater success in all areas of your life.

Critical Thinking: The ability to analyze and evaluate information to make sound decisions is a valuable skill in all areas of life.

To develop good critical thinking, it is important to start with a clear and rational mindset. This means approaching situations with an open mind, being willing to consider alternative perspectives and ideas, and avoiding emotional bias. It is also important to have a systematic approach to evaluating information, assessing evidence, and identifying assumptions and biases. This can involve asking questions, evaluating the validity of sources, and analyzing the logic behind arguments. Another key aspect of critical thinking is the ability to make reasoned judgments and decisions based on evidence, rather than relying solely on intuition or personal preference. This involves being able to identify and weigh competing options, and to evaluate the potential risks and benefits of different courses of action. Ultimately, developing good critical thinking requires practice, reflection, and an ongoing commitment to continuous learning and improvement.

Time Management: The ability to manage one's time effectively is important for achieving goals and balancing various aspects of life.

Here's a tip to help you manage your time better: create a to-do list or schedule. By organizing your tasks and allocating time for each one, you can prioritize your workload and increase productivity. Start by identifying your most important and urgent tasks and scheduling time for them first. Then, allocate time for less important or more time-consuming tasks accordingly. You can also break down larger tasks into smaller, more manageable parts to avoid feeling overwhelmed. It's important to be realistic about the time required for each task and to avoid overloading your schedule. By using a to-do list or schedule, you can better manage your time and accomplish your goals more efficiently.

Problem Solving: The ability to identify problems and develop effective solutions is a valuable skill in both personal and professional life.

You can develop better problem-solving skills by starting with a structured approach that breaks down complex issues into smaller, more manageable parts. One effective method is the '5 Whys' technique, where you ask a series of five questions that get to the root of the problem. By understanding the underlying causes of an issue, you can come up with more effective solutions.

Here's an example:

Problem: A company's website is not generating enough traffic

Why is the website not generating enough traffic?
Answer: The website does not have enough high-quality content.

Why does the website not have enough high-quality content?
Answer: The content team is stretched too thin, and there are not enough resources to produce more content.

Why is the content team stretched too thin?
Answer: There is a high demand for content, and the team is not large enough to keep up.

Why is there a high demand for content?
Answer: The marketing team is running multiple campaigns simultaneously, and each requires unique content.

Why is the marketing team running multiple campaigns simultaneously?
Answer: The company does not have a clear marketing strategy in place, and different departments are working on their own initiatives.

In this example, the root cause of the problem is that the company lacks a clear marketing strategy. By using the '5 Whys' technique, the company can address the underlying issue and implement a more effective solution.

Another helpful approach is to create a decision matrix, which involves listing out all the options and weighing them against specific criteria.

An example:

Let's say you're trying to decide which job offer to accept, and you have three options: Job A, Job B, and Job C. You have identified four criteria that are important to you: salary, commute time, job responsibilities, and company culture. You decide to create a decision matrix to help you compare the options.

First, create a table with the criteria as columns and the options as rows. Your table might look something like this:

Criteria	Job A	Job B	Job C
Salary	$75k	$80k	$70k
Commute	30 min	45 min	1 hr
Job Resp.	Manage	Design	Develop
Culture	Casual	Formal	Casual

Next, assign a weight to each criterion to reflect its importance. For example, you might decide that salary is the most important, so you give it a weight of 4 out of 5. Commute time might be less important to you, so you give it a weight of 2 out of 5. You might assign weights as follows:

Criteria	Weight
Salary	4
Commute	2
Job Resp.	3
Culture	1

Then, score each option for each criterion on a scale of 1-5, with 5 being the best. For example, you might give Job A a score of 4 for salary, 5 for commute time, 3 for job responsibilities, and 4 for company culture. Your scores might look like this:

Criteria	Job A	Job B	Job C
Salary	4	5	3
Commute	5	3	2
Job Resp.	3	4	5
Culture	4	2	4

Finally, multiply the score for each option by the weight for each criterion, and add up the products to get a total score for each option. The option with the highest total score is the one that best meets your criteria. Your totals might look like this:

Option	Total Score
Job A	26
Job B	23
Job C	16

Based on this decision matrix, you would choose Job A, as it has the highest total score.

This can help you make more objective and informed decisions. Finally, it's important to be open to new and creative solutions, even if they are unconventional or outside of your comfort zone. By practicing these techniques, you can become a more confident and effective problem solver in both your personal and professional life.

Financial Management: The ability to manage one's finances effectively is essential for financial stability and long-term success.

The first thing to do to manage your finances well is to establish a budget. Start by calculating your income and expenses to determine how much money you have left over each month. Then, set financial goals for yourself, such as paying off debt or saving for a vacation. It's also important to track your spending and make adjustments as needed to stay within your budget.

Another key aspect of financial management is investing for the future, whether that be through a retirement plan or other types of investments. It's important to research and understand the different investment options available and consult with a financial advisor if necessary.

Leadership: The ability to inspire and guide others is important in personal and professional life.

A simple trick to immediately increase your charisma and leadership is to practice active listening. When you are speaking with someone, give them your undivided attention and focus on what they are saying. Make eye contact, nod your head, and ask questions to show that you are interested in their perspective. This not only makes the other person feel valued and heard, but it also helps you gain important insights and build stronger relationships. Active listening is a key skill for effective communication and leadership, and it can be practiced in both personal and professional settings.

Adaptability: The ability to adapt to new situations and learn new skills is important in a rapidly changing world.

Adaptation is a key skill in today's ever-changing world, and it must occur both internally and externally. Internally, adaptability means having the mental flexibility and resilience to adjust your thoughts and emotions to new situations. Externally, adaptability means having the ability to adjust your actions and behaviors to fit new circumstances. To develop adaptability, it is important to cultivate a growth mindset and embrace change, rather than fearing it. This can involve seeking out new experiences and challenges, being open to feedback and constructive criticism, and learning new skills. Additionally, developing strong problem-solving skills and the ability to think creatively can also help you adapt to new situations more effectively.

Self-Discipline: The ability to stay focused and motivated to achieve goals is essential for success in all areas of life.

Here are 3 ways to develop your self-discipline today:

Start small: Choose a small habit or routine that you want to develop, and commit to doing it every day for a set period of time. This could be something as simple as making your bed in the morning or going for a short walk. By starting with a small goal, you'll build momentum and confidence that will help you tackle bigger challenges.

Practice mindfulness: Self-discipline requires focus and self-awareness. Mindfulness practices like meditation or deep breathing can help you become more aware of your thoughts and feelings, and develop greater control over them. Set aside a few minutes each day to practice mindfulness and observe how it affects your ability to stay disciplined.

Set clear goals: Self-discipline is much easier when you have a clear sense of what you're working towards. Set specific, measurable goals for yourself, and break them down into smaller, achievable steps. This will give you a sense of purpose and direction, and help you stay motivated even when faced with challenges or setbacks.

Creativity: The ability to think outside the box and come up with innovative ideas is valuable in personal and professional life.

The human brain is wired to be creative, and we all possess a natural ability to think outside the box. However, as we grow older, our creativity often gets suppressed due to various factors like societal norms, fear of failure, and pressure to conform. To tap into our creativity, we need to break free from these self-imposed limitations and allow ourselves to think and act without judgment or inhibition.

One way to do this is to rekindle the childlike curiosity and wonder that we all once had. Children are naturally curious and open-minded, unafraid to ask questions and explore the unknown. By adopting a child's mindset, we can begin to see the world from a fresh perspective, to look beyond what is and consider what could be.

Another way to spark our creativity is to engage in activities that stimulate our imagination, such as drawing, painting, writing, or playing music. These activities allow us to express ourselves freely, without worrying about whether our ideas are "good" or "bad." They also help us to develop a habit of regularly engaging in creative endeavors, which in turn, helps to cultivate our creativity over time.

Finally, we can boost our creativity by surrounding ourselves with other creative individuals who inspire and challenge us. By collaborating with others who share our passion for creativity, we can exchange ideas, perspectives, and insights, which can help us to see the world in new and exciting ways.

In summary, by recognizing and tapping into our innate creativity, adopting a childlike mindset, engaging in creative activities, and collaborating with other creatives, we can unleash our full creative potential and lead a more fulfilling life.

Emotional Intelligence: The ability to understand and manage one's emotions and those of others is important for healthy relationships and effective communication.

Emotional intelligence is a crucial skill for success and well-being in all aspects of life. It's the ability to identify, understand, and manage one's own emotions and the emotions of others. We have already talked about the importance of emotional intelligence in relationships, communication, and leadership, but it's worth emphasizing its significance in personal growth and development.

Emotional intelligence can help us better understand and cope with our emotions, leading to better mental health and overall well-being. It can also help us manage stress, resolve conflicts, and make better decisions. Developing emotional intelligence involves a range of skills, such as self-awareness, empathy, self-regulation, and social skills. By practicing these skills, we can improve our emotional intelligence and enhance our personal and professional lives.

Contribute to something larger than yourself

Contributing to something larger than oneself is a critical component of a meaningful life. It is the idea that our existence is not only about personal fulfillment but also about something greater than ourselves. It could be a community, a cause, a movement, or even a larger objective that makes the world a better place. Such contributions can be in the form of time, money, or expertise.

One of the most significant benefits of contributing to something larger than oneself is the sense of purpose it provides. When we work towards a goal that is beyond our individual interests, we feel more connected to the world around us. We begin to see ourselves as part of something more extensive and meaningful, and that understanding can be incredibly fulfilling.

Moreover, contributing to a larger cause can bring a sense of perspective to our lives. It can help us realize that some of the things we worry about are insignificant in the grand scheme of things. It also helps us appreciate our own lives and what we have. We begin to understand that our problems are minor compared to what others may be going through.

Additionally, contributing to something larger than oneself can be an opportunity to connect with other people. It allows us to work with like-minded individuals and forge deeper connections with people who share our values. These connections can be meaningful and last a lifetime.

One example of contributing to something larger than oneself is volunteering. Volunteering can be a powerful way to give back to society and improve the lives of others. It can be done through a wide variety of organizations and causes, such as animal shelters, food banks, hospitals, environmental groups, and so on. Volunteering can provide individuals with the opportunity to work with others who share similar interests, learn new skills, and give back to the community in a meaningful way.

Another example is philanthropy. Charitable giving to causes that align with one's values can be a way of making a difference and contributing to something larger than oneself. This can take many forms, from donating to a specific charity to supporting a cause through fundraising or activism. Philanthropy can help individuals feel a sense of accomplishment and purpose and make a tangible difference in the world.

Yes, contributing to something larger than oneself is one of the most important points for a fulfilling life. It can bring a sense of purpose, perspective, and connection to others, and allow individuals to make a meaningful impact on the world. Whether through volunteering, philanthropy, or other means, we can all find ways to contribute and make a difference in the world around us.

Conclusion

As we come to the end of this book, I hope that the insights and ideas we have shared have been helpful in your personal growth and development journey. Remember that self-improvement is a continuous process, and you have the power to transform your life by implementing the tips and practices discussed in this book.

I encourage you to leave a comment online sharing your thoughts on this book and how it has helped you. Your feedback can be valuable to others who are seeking to improve their lives, and it will also motivate us to continue creating helpful content.

Thank you for taking the time to read this book, and I wish you all the best in your personal growth journey. Remember to keep practicing the tips and techniques outlined in this book, and don't hesitate to reach out for help or guidance when you need it.